Watch It Grow
Snake
Barrie Watts

Smart Apple Media

First published in 2002 by Franklin Watts
96 Leonard Street, London EC2A 4XD, United Kingdom
Franklin Watts Australia, 56 O'Riordan Street, Alexandria, NSW 2015
Copyright © 2002 Barrie Watts

Editor: Adrian Cole, Art director: Jonathan Hair, Photographer: Barrie
Watts, Illustrator: David Burroughs, Consultant: Beverley Mathias, REACH
Picture credits: page 28, Geoff Trinder/Ardea London

Published in the United States by Smart Apple Media
1980 Lookout Drive, North Mankato, Minnesota 56003

U.S. publication copyright © 2003 Smart Apple Media

Library of Congress Cataloging-in-Publication Data

Watts, Barrie. Snake / Barrie Watts. p. cm. — (Watch it grow)
Summary: A simple introduction to the physical characteristics and
behavior of snakes, emphasizing their birth and development.
ISBN 1-58340-200-4 1. Snakes—Life cycles—Juvenile literature.
[1. Snakes. 2. Animals—Infancy.] I. Title.
QL666.06 W323 2002   597.96—dc21   2002017024

2 4 6 8 9 7 5 3

How to use this book

Watch It Grow has been specially designed to cater to a
range of reading and learning abilities. Initially, children may
just follow the pictures. Ask them to describe in their own
words what they see. Other children will enjoy reading the
single sentence in large type in conjunction with the pictures.
This single sentence is then expanded in the main text.
More adept readers will be able to follow the text and pictures
by themselves through to the conclusion of the snake's life
cycle. **Please note:** A Carolina corn snake (*Elaphe guttata),*
used as the subject for this book, does not reflect the
growth or behavior of all types of snakes.

Contents

Snakes come from eggs.

Snake eggs are about one inch (2.5 cm) long and have a soft, leathery shell. Inside each egg, a baby snake is growing. A female snake lays her eggs in the spring. She may lay as many as 20 eggs.

The eggs are laid in a hole in damp soil. The soil keeps the eggs warm so the baby snakes can grow.

The baby snake grows inside.

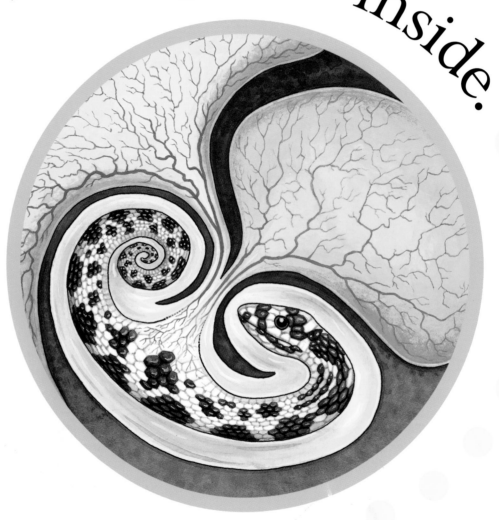

The eggs take about 10 weeks to hatch. Inside each egg, the baby snake eats the egg yolk. This helps it to grow strong.

The baby snake breathes air through tiny holes in the eggshell. When it is ready to hatch, the snake cuts through the tough shell with its **egg tooth**.

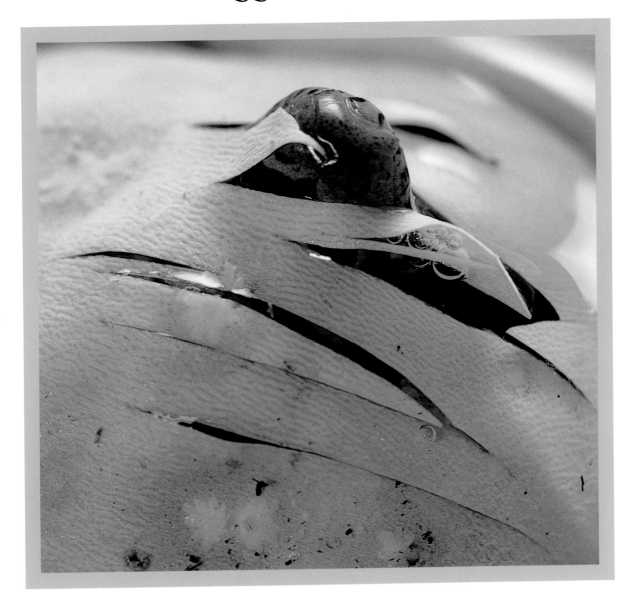

The snake hatches.

The snake pushes its head out of the egg. It looks like its parents but is a different color and is much smaller in size.

When the snake hatches, it is only as big as a pencil. By the time it is fully grown, it may be more than 6.5 feet (2 m) long.

The baby snake looks after itself.

The snake can swim and climb as soon as it hatches.

It must catch its own food and avoid **predators**. It has to be very careful, as some birds, mammals, and even other snakes would like to eat it.

11

The baby snake has its first meal.

Two or three days after hatching, the baby snake begins looking for food. It usually waits until it is dark.

The baby snake mainly
eats animals that are
slow-moving and easy
to catch. It often eats
young birds and mice
that are still in their nest.

The snake sheds its skin.

Two weeks after hatching, the young
snake has grown too big for its old skin.
A new skin grows under the old one.

The snake turns a dull color
and its eyes become cloudy.
It is ready to **molt**.
The snake rubs itself against a
rough stone. This helps it wriggle
out of the old
skin, which it
then leaves
behind.

The snake
will molt
many more
times during
its life.

The snake changes its skin color.

The color of the snake's skin changes each time it **molts**. The skin becomes more colorful as the snake grows older.

Once it is fully grown, the snake pictured in this book will have brown skin with red patches on it. These colors **camouflage** the snake from **predators**.

The snake lives on sandy
ground among leaves,
rocks, and fallen branches.
It can hide very easily.

The snake can move quickly.

After five months, the snake has doubled in size. It has a long backbone made up of more than 200 small bones. The joints are stretchy and bend easily.

The snake can race over the ground using its powerful muscles in an "S" motion. It grips the ground with its belly **scales**. It can move about as fast as a child can run.

The snake basks in the sun.

The snake, like all **reptiles**, is cold-blooded. This means its blood temperature changes with hot or cold weather. If the snake is cold, it cannot move quickly enough to catch food.

The snake must warm itself by
basking in the sun. Its **scales**
keep it from drying out.
When the snake is warm
enough, it looks for food.

The snake hunts for food.

The snake does not have good eyesight, but it does have a good sense of smell. Its forked tongue picks up scents and carries them to a special sense organ in the snake's mouth called **Jacobson's Organ.**

When the snake hunts, it uses its tongue to follow the scent trails left by **prey**.

The snake
catches a meal.

The snake uses its teeth to catch its **prey**. Here it has caught a large mouse. The snake coils its body around the prey and kills it by **constriction**.

The snake cannot chew its prey. Instead, it uses powerful throat and jaw muscles to swallow it whole, head first.

The snake sleeps through the winter.

After seven months, as winter approaches, the snake finds a place to **hibernate**. It looks for a hollow in a tree or a hole under a rock. It must sleep through the winter in order to survive the cold.

During hibernation, the snake's heartbeat slows down and its blood temperature becomes colder. It uses its body fat as food to stay alive.

The female snake lays her eggs.

In early spring, the snake emerges from **hibernation**. It spends a few days **basking** in the sun. An adult male snake uses his sense of smell to find a female and mates with her. Soon after mating, the female snake lays her eggs.

The female snake makes a hole in warm, damp soil and pushes the eggs out of an opening in her body one by one. She may lay some more later in a different place. When she has laid her eggs, she leaves the baby snakes to hatch by themselves.

Word bank

Basking - when a snake lies in the sun to warm up its cold blood so it can move around quickly.

Camouflage - when the color and pattern of an animal's skin is similar to its surroundings, so it is hard to see. Camouflage helps an animal to hide.

Constriction - when a snake coils its body around an animal and squeezes it to stop its breathing.

Egg tooth - a small tooth used by a baby snake to break through the shell of its egg. It disappears shortly after birth.

Hibernate - when an animal hides and goes into a deep sleep for the winter because the weather is too cold.

Jacobson's Organ - an organ found on the roof of a snake's mouth that helps the snake to sense smells.

Molt - when a snake sheds its skin.

Predators - meat-eating animals. Snake's predators include some birds, mammals, and other snakes.

Prey - any animal that is hunted for food by another animal.

Reptiles - the group of scaly, cold-blooded animals that includes snakes, crocodiles, and tortoises.

Scales - small, hard plates that cover a snake's whole body.

Life cycle

Ten weeks after the eggs are laid, the baby snake hatches.

In early spring, after mating, an adult female snake lays her own eggs.

The baby snake can swim and climb. It must look after itself.

When winter approaches, the snake hibernates.

Two weeks after hatching, the snake sheds its skin for the first time.

The snake kills its prey by constriction and then swallows it whole.

The snake's skin color changes as it gets older. Its color helps it to hide.

After five months, the snake has doubled in size. It moves quickly using its belly scales.

Index